THE WORLD CA...
ST. LOUIS

A Visit to the 1904 World's Fair

Dorothy Daniels Birk

Foreword by August A. Busch, Jr.

Chalice Press

St. Louis, Missouri

Cover and Text Design by Shelley Dieterichs

© **1979 Dorothy Daniels Birk**

12 11 10 9 8 7   **97 98 99 00 01 02**

Library of Congress Cataloging in Publication Data
Birk, Dorothy Daniels.
The world came to St. Louis.
   Includes index.
    1. St. Louis. Louisiana Purchase Exposition, 1904.
I. Title.
T860.B1B57   909.82′1′074017866   79-10396
ISBN 0-8272-4213-1

Printed in the United States of America

Foreword

The book you are about to read is, I think, much more than it purports to be.

It is essentially the story of the Louisiana Purchase Exposition, from its conception in the fertile minds of St. Louis' "city fathers" to the closing night ceremonies on December 1, 1904. It is a thoroughly researched historical document filled with thousands of facts; and yet, unlike many historical works, the book is easy and enjoyable reading.

Part of the reason for this is a delightful profusion of excellent illustrations of the buildings and personalities of the Fair. The other reason for its readability is, I suspect, the fact that the book's "parent" was an audiovisual presentation—an illustrated lecture, if you will—in which Dorothy Birk literally talks one through the entire fabulous Fair. It is this style of chatty commentary, rather than ponderous historical data, which contributes so much to the reader's enjoyment.

The author was born and reared in St. Louis. It is her city, and she has great pride in it. She decries its detractors, applauds its boosters and yearns for the "glory days" of the turn of the century.

It is this theme of pride and challenge in the book that particularly interests me, that provides the added dimension I spoke of at the beginning.

St. Louis is my town too, and my ancestors'. I am proud of it, too. In my own way I have tried to do what I can for its improvement, its redevelopment and its pride. In this little volume I see a challenge to the citizens of St. Louis to continue the vitality, the creativity and the civic pride which has made us one of the great cities of the world.

Let me cite just a few examples from the book which should provoke the imagination of every reader. In 1904, St. Louis was the fourth largest city in the country. Its central location on two great rivers made it the absolute hub of both rail and river traffic. It had an early start in the industrial revolution, with manufacturing and commerce considering it a prime location.

Today, on the 75th anniversary of the Great Fair, St. Louis is again on the threshold of an era of growth, redevelopment and prosperity. It is a perfectly appropriate point in time during which we might pause and take pride in and guidance from the glories of our municipal past.

Shortly after the idea for the 1904 Fair was conceived, it was recognized that $15,000,000 would be needed to get it off the ground. One third of that, it was determined, should come from individual citizens, "the man on the street," partly because that was the only way the total could be achieved and partly to ensure the total involvement of the populace in the huge endeavor. All this, of course, was in 1903, when a dollar was many times harder to come by than it is today.

It is a tremendous testimonial to St. Louisans of 1903—and a challenge to all of us today—that such a goal was set and reached to make the Fair a reality.

I commend the book to you so that you may relive the glory of the single most significant happening in the history of St. Louis. And I do so with the hope that the inherent challenges in it will continue to be met, keeping our city at the level it enjoyed when "The World Came to St. Louis."

August A. Busch, Jr.

Contents

Dedicated
to the memory of my father,
Edward S. Daniels,
whose love and enthusiasm for the Fair
and whose outstanding talent
in photography
have given me a challenging heritage

Preface ''The Birth of a Show''

It seems that for years, whenever my parents and their friends were together the conversation always came around to the ''marvelous, fabulous'' St. Louis World's Fair! They would reminisce and rave: ''Wasn't it beautiful—and huge!'' ''Those Palaces—and Festival Hall atop Art Hill!'' ''The Ferris Wheel!'' And on and on, always ending, ''Let's get out Ed's slides and go to the Fair again!'' (Ed was my father, Edward S. Daniels.) So, you see, I was exposed to the Fair at a very young age.

As I grew older I sadly realized that many St. Louisans are anything but St. Louis-boosters. Then why was there such lasting enthusiasm about the Fair? After I married I began to understand. My husband, Julian Birk, loved photography and was fascinated by my dad's big (3¼'' x 4'') double-glass slides. History repeated itself! Our friends were frequently exposed to the slides of the Fair, about 140 slides altogether, and our generation began to exclaim, ''The Fair was so different from those of today!''

By 1967 word had spread about my having a ''big box full'' of original slides taken at the Fair. Eventually the word reached the ears of Bernice Mocker, president of the University City People to People group to which I belong. (People to People, an organization founded by President Eisenhower after World War II, works at building a firm foundation for world peace by encouraging increased communication and, therefore, improved understanding among ''ordinary'' people throughout the world.) Bernice asked me to present a show for our group, since after all, what could be more ''people to people'' than a World's Fair?

I agreed and then realized that, as many times as I had seen the slides, I couldn't even identify the buildings. A close friend, Ginnie Horner, hearing of my problem, offered to help. It was an offer I accepted with both alacrity and great appreciation.

Then another problem arose. The projector I had to show the slides, originally lighted with kerosene and later adapted to use a small electric bulb, would never be adequate for use in a large hall. Again fate came to the rescue. The University City Chamber of Commerce directed me to Robert Norvell, who had a 1908 Bausch and Lomb projector which he was willing to lend to me. So, the show could go on.

Research began. Ginnie researched the buildings and I researched the human interest aspects. I had expected to look through two or three books for enough material for one program, but I got "hooked" on this amazing happening in St. Louis in 1904. I'm still reading everything about the Fair I can lay my hands on. The problem is that the more I read, the harder it becomes to leave something out of a show—I could talk all night.

Since that first show in September 1967, I have given hundreds of shows to thousands of people. In the fall of 1978, Bethany Press asked if I would be interested in developing a book based on my show, combining both my script and the pictures. They felt the book would be a permanent record of my show and an excellent way to commemorate the 75th anniversary of the Fair. The project sounded interesting and the people at Bethany Press were very excited, so we got to work and created this book.

The enthusiastic reception at the shows and the interest in this book, as well as in the Fair itself, still amaze me. I hope that all this enthusiasm will, in the words of David R. Francis, the president of the Fair, "kindle deep civic pride and incite to noble effort many public-minded citizens"—citizens dedicated to a dream for St. Louis and resolutely committed to making their dream come true. Oh, what miracles could happen to this wonderful St. Louis of ours!

Dorothy Daniels Birk
April 1979

8

THE WORLD CAME TO ST. LOUIS

Genius points.
Inspiration whispers,
"Nothing Impossible."

Dedicated to Accomplishment

Are you ready to go back? Back to the never-again land of the St. Louis World's Fair, 1904? Known as the Louisiana Purchase Exposition because it was to commemorate the 100th anniversary of the Louisiana Purchase, the Fair lasted seven fabulous months in St. Louis, from April 30 through December 1. The Fair was a festival of music, art, architecture and landscaping all combined into one unified whole, the likes of which had never been seen before and have never been seen since.

Let's think a moment about the days of 1904. Life was very different from today. For instance, a shave cost a nickel. A bath in a porcelain tub (and it was something to be able to take a bath in a porcelain tub in 1904) was fifteen cents. And liquor was five cents for "a paralyzing glassful." St. Louis' major claim to fame in 1904 was caskets, shoes and beer. We were the fourth largest city in the United States.

The Fair was an almost unbelievable combination of three things: amazing individuals, a very different idea for a fair, and a fantastic execution of that idea.

Let's discuss the people first. They were headed by David R. Francis—and what a man he must have been! He had served as mayor of St. Louis and governor of Missouri, and had also worked in the Depart-

David R. Francis

11

ment of the Interior of the United States government. He eventually became Ambassador to Russia and was a member of the Board of Trustees of Washington University, just to name a few of his accomplishments. He gathered around him a remarkable group of men. They were fearless, tireless, daring, and dauntless. They had a dream—a dream for a fair in St. Louis that could never again be duplicated. And they were determined that this dream would come true and that *nothing* would stop them. This was their motto: "Nothing will divert us, nothing will deter us, there is *nothing* that we cannot and will not accomplish." With that kind of dedication, the dream was certain to become a reality.

It was determined very early that a backlog of 15 million dollars was needed, and that the *people* of St. Louis—not only the VIPs and the big business men, but the people in the streets—had to get behind the idea of a World's Fair in St. Louis and be willing to dig into their pockets to put up 5 million dollars. Then the city would put up 5 million and the national government another 5 million, giving the planners this backlog of 15 million dollars. So, Mr. Francis' group formed a committee of 200 persons who punched doorbells throughout St. Louis; they sold shares in the Fair for ten dollars each and in just a few months, they had almost 5 million dollars.

The second thing that made the Fair so outstanding was the aim, the idea, the scope of the Fair. It was to be a living, working, university of man—his work and his world, his progress to that day, and (here is where it differs from any other World's Fair) the meaning and potential of all this for humanity. In other words, "Here is where we stand today in 1904 in all the fields of science. How do we best go forward in each of these fields for the ultimate good of mankind?" For this purpose scientists were brought to St. Louis from all over the world. The roster read like a scientific "Who's Who" of 1904. They met together in Congresses all over the metropolitan area: in the old Coliseum, in apartments, in hotels, in the palaces on the Fairgrounds, and in the dormitories of Washington University. The scientists actually studied, researched, and experimented here, making many wonderful discoveries as a result of their efforts.

The third thing that made the Fair so outstanding was the actual execution of the "university" idea. It was to be a dream come true, done with great imagination. The palaces were to be the largest, the avenues the broadest, and the vistas the grandest, in a setting of art, music and architecture created by the most talented artists and artisans in the world. The tone for the Fair was set by President McKinley's proclamation to the rulers of the world: "I do hereby invite the nations of the earth to appoint representatives and send such exhibits as will most fittingly and fully illustrate their resources, their industries and their progress in civilization."

One of the first things that the Fair Fathers (David R. Francis and his group) did was to appoint a press and publicity committee. This committee worked unceasingly and imaginatively, putting out over 3½ million pieces of publicity in the first six months, printed in (Can you imagine this in prosaic old St. Louis?) German, French, Spanish, Portuguese and Italian. St. Louis had nine newspapers at the time; six of them were German, each printing an average of more than twenty-eight columns about the Fair daily for three years. There were two morning newspapers, each of which printed an average of five columns daily about the Fair.

In the beginning, the idea for a World's Fair in St. Louis was very modest. The Fair Fathers originally said, "Let's hold it on one block of the riverfront, the block to be bounded by the river, Main Street, Walnut and Market." But after second thoughts, they agreed: "We can't do justice to this idea in just one block. Maybe we'd better use the whole riverfront." This would have called for condemnation proceedings and would have meant a great deal of work. The city fathers would have had to write an ordinance, get public opinion behind it, and marshall the vote to pass it. But, with their determination, Francis' committee was willing to do all this if necessary.

About this time the press caught on to the possibility of a fair here. Even some officials in Washington became enthusiastic about the fair. A few big business

The northwest corner of Forest Park was known as the Wilderness. It was "in a state of demoralized nature, unsewered, unwatered, unlighted, unimproved."

men began saying, "I think you've got something here. I'll put up so much money whether there is profit in it or not." For this was the logical place to hold a World's Fair to commemorate the 100th anniversary of the Louisiana Purchase. St. Louis had been the seat of both the Spanish and French governments of the Ter-

13

ritory. It had also been the actual site of the transfer of the upper Louisiana Territory. Since President Jefferson had said that the Louisiana Purchase was second in influence and importance only to the Declaration of Independence, the committee decided to go "all out."

The Fair Fathers decided to hold the fair in the west half of Forest Park. But that didn't give them enough room. So, for $750,000 they leased the entire Washington University campus, which included several buildings that were to be ready for use by the time of the Fair. That still wasn't enough room, so the group leased land to the south of the campus, from Forsyth all the way to Clayton Road. Another small piece of land was added, roughly from Lindell and De Baliviere north to the Wabash railroad tracks. This gave the Fair Fathers a rectangular area extending from De Baliviere on the east to Big Bend on the west, and from the Wabash tracks on the north to Oakland Avenue on the south. Altogether this amounted to 1,240 acres—still one of the largest acreages of any World's Fair.

The Fair Fathers felt that they owed the people of St. Louis something special, since these were the ones who had dug into their pockets and put up 5 million dollars. Therefore, they decided to hold several ceremonies symbolizing the progress of the Fair, hoping to give the people of St. Louis, from the very beginning, the idea that this was "their" Fair. The first ceremony

The stake and hatchet used in the ceremony of the first stake, September 3, 1901, were donated to the Missouri Historical Society.

was held in September 1901, when the first stake was driven into the ground at a point a little to the southwest of the Art Museum as we know it today. This was to be the focal point of the Fair, from which the main avenues would radiate like the ribs of a woman's fan. Although David R. Francis was a very punctual man, he was so late for this ceremony that those present became alarmed and sent out a search party. Mr. Francis and his party had been lost in the "wilds" of Forest Park!

Straightening the River Des Peres. 110,000 cubic yards of dirt were moved for the new channel. The entire job was to be completed within 65 days with a penalty of $150 for each extra day.

Another ceremony was that of the ground breaking, in December of 1901. The state governors and national figures braved ten-below-zero weather and a five-inch snow for this event; the ground was frozen so hard that they had to use a pick to make a dent in it. The three shovels used for the ceremony were the Shapleigh Hardware shovel, which was silver and ebony; a shovel of 1803 which was, of course, the date of the Purchase; and a French Lamotte shovel, the kind used by lead miners 200 years before.

One of the first things the engineers had to do was to straighten the River Des Peres. "She was a crooked little stream," they said, "that wandered over the park like a dog smelling trees. So we filled in some of it and put the rest in a wooden box 4,600 feet long."

Part of the Fair Fathers' dream was that the palaces would be the largest. This was the beginning of the age of steel but, had the output of all the steel mills in the country been used, there still would not have been enough steel to build even the eight main palaces. Since the Fair Fathers had decided very early that all construction should be alike, they used wood for the palaces—long-leaf yellow pine.

Some of the palaces had nine miles of aisles between the booths. One really had to have good feet and strong shoes, or rather, strong feet and good shoes. Roofing paper was placed over the wooden construction; then over this was put a material called staff. Staff was a kind of plaster mixed with a special fiber which had been imported from Manila especially for the World's Fair buildings.

The Fair Fathers had some qualms abut the durability of staff. It was a new material; would it last the seven months of changeable St. Louis weather? A work crew of two men was appointed to watch for and report immediately any sign of deterioration. The Fair Fathers would then get together whatever

15

To help get an idea of the size of the palaces: An average of 18 trains of 40 cars each (a total of 720 cars) would be needed to carry the materials—the wood, plaster, sand, fiber, glass, nails, and paint—to build one palace.

Applying the "staff" used in the construction of the palaces.

size work crew was necessary to keep everything in order. This job didn't keep the two men very busy! Staff proved to be durable beyond their wildest imaginings!

About this time St. Louisans began to get into the habit of packing a picnic lunch and going over to the park after church on Sunday, to see how "their" Fair was getting along. At this stage of the Fair's development, David R. Francis made a trip to Europe—a big undertaking in 1901—and personally called on the rulers of England, France, Germany, Spain and Belgium, to try to persuade them to exhibit at the St. Louis World's Fair.

April 30, 1903 was to have been the opening day of the Fair. This was the actual 100th anniversary of the Louisiana Purchase, but the Fair Fathers saw very early that with their grandiose ideas, the Fair was not going to be ready. They wisely decided, "Well, we have already announced the day, so let's keep it and call it Dedication Day. Then we can have Opening Day services a year later, on April 30, 1904."

It was easy to recognize President Teddy Roosevelt when he appeared on the reviewing stand. Although it was President McKinley who had sent the proclamation of the Fair to the rulers of the world, his assassination at the Buffalo Exposition of 1901 had put Roosevelt in the White House. One easily can imagine the precautions that were then taken for President Roosevelt's life: a special train ran ten minutes ahead of the President's train from Washington; special tracks were constructed onto the Fairgrounds, up to the Palace of Transportation, where the engine was kept at full steam all the time he was here. Thank goodness there were no incidents!

Holding Dedication Day services a year ahead of Opening Day proved to be one of the wisest things the Fair Fathers could have done. The tens of thousands of visitors who poured into St. Louis for Dedication Day revealed many weak spots in the Fair's planning, and the city thus had a full year to overcome these weaknesses. Good old St. Louis really rolled up her sleeves and went to work. A few examples: (1) It was found that some carriage, cab and hack drivers had charged exorbitant prices. So an ordinance was passed which named a fair price and not only required drivers to show proof of cooperation, but also gave police the right to arrest them if they didn't. (2) It was found that hotel accommodations were completely inadequate, so dozens of projects were formed to relieve this. Some apartments became temporary hotels. Some St. Louis businessmen again came forward and said, "I still believe in what you are doing; I'll put up so much more money whether there will be profit in it or not." And some businessmen came forward with incentives. Adolphus Busch of Anheuser-Busch said, "I'll give $50,000 outright to the person who can have a hotel ready in the city of St. Louis for the Fair and another $50,000 to the one

Dedication Day, April 30, 1903. Grover Cleveland is shown on the left and Theodore Roosevelt in the center. Also on the reviewing stand were David R. Francis and the "Fair Fathers," various members of Congress, the Cabinet, the Supreme Court, foreign ministers and ambassadors, representatives of the Army and the Navy, and the Board of Lady Managers.

who can have one ready in the county for the Fair." (3) It was also found that transportation was completely inadequate, so the railroads, which had been

Opening Day, April 30, 1904, was proclaimed a public holiday. 187,793 were in attendance at 1:06 P.M. to watch David R. Francis signal President Roosevelt in Washington that everything was ready. Roosevelt pushed a button that started the machinery at the Fair and the Fair was officially opened.

highly competitive, resolved their problems and gave service such as we today would envy. A quick example: On weekends a train would leave Union Station *every minute* for the Fairgrounds. If this were possible

in 1904, think of what we could do today—if we had the *will!*

Let's move on to Opening Day, April 30, 1904. There had been a violent twelve-hour snowstorm on April 20 and the Fair Fathers almost had hysterics: "What will we do if this continues?" But St. Louis weather is so changeable and unpredictable that by April 30, Opening Day dawned beautiful and spring-like. The services were brief and dignified. Nearly two hundred thousand people were there to hear David R. Francis open the Fair with these words: "Open ye gates, swing wide ye portals, enter herein ye sons of men," (and here's where it differs from other World's Fairs) "learn the lessons here taught and gather from it inspiration for still greater accomplishments." With those words a plunger was pressed in the East Room of the White House in Washington, which unfurled the flags and set in motion the mighty engines. A dream had come true, for Forest Park had been transformed from wilderness to wonderland. The Fair was open after six years of work; it had taken ten to twenty thousand workers to build fifteen hundred separate buildings representing all the states and territories, plus forty-five nations.

The Fairgrounds were open from 8:00 in the morning until 11:30 P.M. The palaces opened at 9:00 and closed at sunset, but occasionally the Art Palace and the Palace of Electricity would remain open until closing time. Admission to the Fair cost fifty cents. Of course,

The Jefferson Guard was comprised of a minimum of 300 carefully selected men (more at peak times). They were paid $50 a month and housed in Cupples II on the Washington University campus.

a book of tickets could be bought; the more tickets in the book, the lower the admission price. The Fair Fathers had expected to have the Fair open seven days a week, but very early a ruckus arose about having it open on Sunday. The case went from court to court, the final decision being that the Fair had to be closed on Sunday. This quote from the *Minneapolis Tribune* shows how times have since changed: "The wicked plotting of the directors [of the Fair] has come to naught, and the wicked city of St. Louis will be compelled to respect the Sabbath as it was probably never respected there before." Imagine not even being able to go to a fair on Sunday!

Regardless of where you went on the Fairgrounds, you could always find a Jefferson Guard. These were the police of the Fair, but they were really more than that. Jefferson Guards were charged with three duties: to be guide, philosopher and friend. As guides, they were to introduce visitors to the beauties of the Fair. As philosophers, they were to have absorbed some of the knowledge from these mighty exhibits from all over the world, and help to show Fair-goers the meaning and the possibility of it all—to make it a learning experience. Anyone who had a question could ask a Jefferson Guard for the answer. And as friends, the Guards were to save reckless people from being run over by the intramural train that ran at the terrific speed of twelve miles an hour.

In the following pages we will "tour" the Fairgrounds. We will enter at the main entrance, which was roughly at De Baliviere and Lindell. Then we will go up the main avenue, the Plaza of St. Louis, which becomes a lagoon—the same lagoon that is at the foot of Art Hill today. In fact, all the lagoons in Forest Park were built for the Fair. On the Plaza of St. Louis and around this lagoon we will see the first four of the eight main palaces. Then we'll go up what we now call Art Hill (down which tumbled the Cascades) and up to the "jewel," the gem of the whole Fair—Festival Hall. Next we will turn back and go north up the east avenue, the Avenue of Orleans, and see two more of the main palaces. Then we'll go up the west avenue, the Avenue of St. Anthony, and see palaces seven and eight.

By this time we will have returned to the main entrance near De Baliviere and Lindell, where we will board the intramural train and go west at that terrific speed, roughly along what is now Lindell. On the right will be the Pike, the fun section of the Fair. There was fun all over the Fairgrounds, but the Pike was the part that was dedicated to fun. Then on to the Washington University campus, the Terrace of Forty-five Nations, and through the Department of Anthropology, where fifty-odd tribes were brought from all over the world. Then we will go between Festival Hall and the Art Museum, which was directly behind it, up to the southeast part of the Fairgrounds to see the buildings of the states, and back to our starting point.

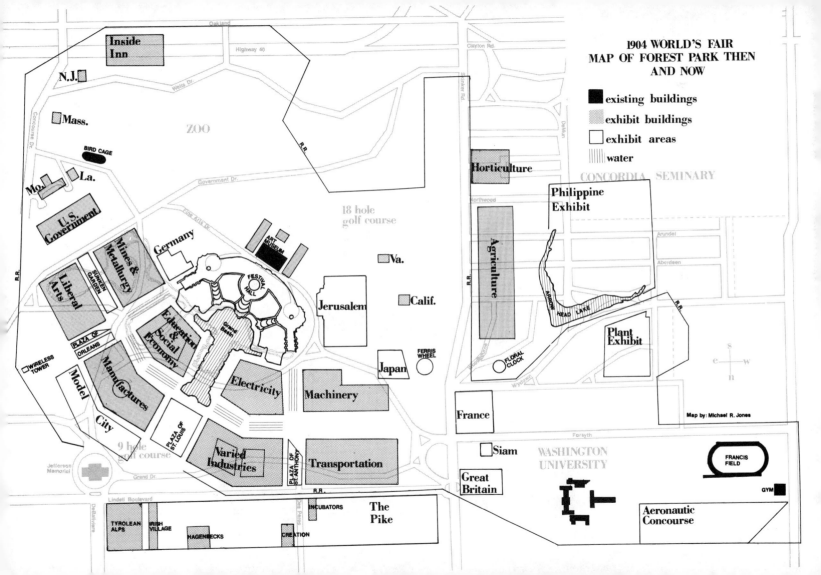

The University of Man

The Statue of St. Louis, honoring Louis IX of France, is considered one of the finest accomplishments of the sculptor Charles H. Niehaus.

Let's go to the Fair! Starting up the Plaza of St. Louis, the first thing that would greet us, fittingly, would be the statue of St. Louis. This statue, made of staff as were all the statues on the Fairgrounds, was cast in bronze after the Fair and is the one we know and love on Art Hill today. The Plaza of St. Louis was the main avenue and was 600 feet wide, in accordance with the Fair Fathers' dream of the broadest avenues. This was the equivalent of twelve average city lots, fifty feet wide each. On one side of the avenue was a statue of DeSoto, who discovered the Mississippi River, and on the other side Joliet, who explored the Mississippi River region. Moving on up the Plaza of St. Louis, we would come to the Louisiana Purchase Monument. This was a shaft 100 feet high. On the top was a statue of Peace, alighting on the globe; the globe was held up by four statues representing the four directions. Around its base were statues depicting memorable events in the history of the Louisiana Territory. (By the way, all the statuary on the Fairgrounds had to be pertinent to the Louisiana Territory: its explorers, discoverers, the nature of the Territory, its folklore, etc.)

A sculptor would submit a small scale model of a statue, hoping it would be selected and then blown up to the enormous size needed for the Fair. Sculpture

The Plaza of St. Louis. On one side was a statue of Ferdinand DeSoto, who discovered the "Father of Waters" while in search of the Fountain of Youth. On the other side was a statue of Louis Joliet, who led an expedition that traced the course of the Mississippi and determined that the river flowed into the Gulf of Mexico and not the Pacific Ocean, as previously thought.

The Louisiana Purchase Monument stood at the south end of the Plaza of St. Louis, at the edge of the Grand Basin.

was judged on two scores. First of all, was it outstanding artistically? Secondly, was it about something pertinent to the Territory? If the statue was accepted on these two scores, the little scale model was then shipped to a factory in the state of New York, where it was blown up to the *enormous* size necessary for it to be in correct proportion to the huge palaces.

After passing the monument, we would come to the first palace, the Palace of Manufactures. Here we would see household articles, equipment, adornment and decoration for personal, domestic, and general use. At the time of the Chicago World's Fair in 1893, only the very rich could purchase the lovely things shipped in from all over the world. But times had changed between 1893 and 1904, and for the St. Louis World's Fair, people of much more moderate circumstances could purchase many things. The United States Customs collected half a million dollars in duty on foreign goods sold here. The Palace of Manufactures was the shopping center of the Fair, and the people of St. Louis loved it. It was their introduction to bazaars and arcades, things which we are used to today—but which were all new to them.

The second palace was the Palace of Varied Industries. Here there were 231 classes of exhibits in 34 groups, covering industrial art, furniture, interiors, jewelry, and artwork. The third palace was the Palace of Education and Social Economy. This building ex-

The Palace of Manufactures as seen from the northwest corner of the Grand Basin.

The Palace of Varied Industries covered 14 acres. Germany and Japan were rivals as to the extent of space in this palace.

The Palace of Education and Social Economy (seen here in construction) housed schools of every variety from kindergarten to the highest university levels. Included were agricultural, commercial, and poly-technical schools, as well as special schools for the deaf, the mute, and the blind.

The Palace of Electricity. One of the "marvels of the electrical age" was "fast food"—sirloin steaks in 6 minutes, chicken roasted in 14 minutes, lobster broiled in 12 minutes, squab in 8. A special broiler cooked a steak on both sides at once! "Exquisite!"

emplified another way in which our Fair differed from any other World's Fair: there were no scale models. Everything was real—real farms, real mines, real bakeries, real schools from all over the world. There were technical schools from Germany, manual schools from Sweden, industrial schools from France, Austria and Italy, and art schools from Austria, Great Britain and Ireland. Think of what a learning experience it was for educators from all over the world to sit together in Congresses: "This is the way we teach reading in our country. How do you do it in yours? What can we learn from you? What can you learn from us?" It was a living, working university of man!

Again, this was the Palace of Education *and* Social Economy. Social Economy was a brand new field. It was the first evidence of the attention of government and people to economic questions and the conditions of industry and labor. In this palace were examples of civic improvement, public health, welfare and progress of mankind, charities and corrections, hygiene, and municipal improvement.

Let's go on to the fourth palace, the Palace of Electricity. This was the beginning of the electrical age. From the Fairgrounds, St. Louis could communicate by wireless with Chicago, Springfield and Kansas City. That sounds almost silly to us today, doesn't it, when we can communicate with the moon? But we must remember that this was a "first" in 1904, and just as wonderful then as our first communication with

A night view of the Louisiana Purchase Monument and Festival Hall.

the moon was to us. Telephone communication was just beginning to become universal, and many St. Louisans had the thrill of hearing, via telephone, the voices of loved ones who lived outside St. Louis. There were examples of messages being recorded on steel wire and then replayed—the first "tape" recorder. Thomas Edison was here to make sure that the electrical exhibits were properly set up. Do you remember the Congresses mentioned earlier, where scientists were brought here to study, research and experiment? The International Electrical Congress was one of the largest and most far-reaching in impact of the Congresses. Little did they dream that we would be taught to use electricity to such an extent that today we wonder where we're going to get enough energy to sustain our extravagant use of it!

From this side of the lagoon, we would see the Louisiana Purchase Monument silhouetted against Festival Hall on the other side. Festival Hall, as previously noted, was the crowning feature of the Fair, the "jewel," the gem—and huge! It was 200 feet from the foundation to the statue on the apex. This statue was Evelyn Longman's "Victorious Athlete." It was interesting to learn that even today small replicas of that huge statue, created for the top of Festival Hall, are used for athletic trophies.

Festival Hall was the axial point from which the three main plazas radiated. It stood immediately in front of the Palace of Fine Arts (now the Art Museum) at the midpoint of the Terrace of States.

In front of Festival Hall the central Cascades gushed from a fountain 20 feet above the terrace, spread to a stream 45 feet wide, and leaped down Art Hill to a width of 150 feet as it poured into the Grand Basin. At night the Cascades were lighted in three alternating colors.

Imagine having had *this* in St. Louis! The dome of Festival Hall was larger than the dome of St. Peter's Basilica in Rome, and was covered with gold leaf. Inside was an auditorium which seated 3,500 people. There was room on the stage for 400 people. Festival Hall contained the largest organ in the world and Charles Galloway, a famous St. Louis organist who lived up the street from me on Magnolia when I was a girl, was the organist in residence. In addition, outstanding organists from all over the world were brought to play on this gorgeous instrument. (After the Fair the organ was dismantled, loaded onto thirteen railroad cars, and moved to Wanamaker's department store in Philadelphia, where it can still be seen and heard today.)

The first Peace Congress in the world was held in beautiful Festival Hall. Two hundred people from fifteen nations met to promote universal peace. After their meeting, they said, ''We advocate, nay, we demand, to lessen the possibility of war, that causes be settled in the same way that cases be settled in the courts of law. Public opinion supports and is in favor of the settlement of international disputes through courts of arbitration.'' Some of us are still working and praying for this today—praying that *someday* we will be ''civilized'' enough to settle our international disputes *not* with our brawn, but with our brain. Since we have proven that we have enough brains to put men on the moon and explore outer space, doesn't it seem that we *can* do anything that we have the *will* to do?!

Completing the beauty of Festival Hall, a series of cascades tumbled down Art Hill and plunged into the Grand Basin. The Cascades make me think of the quality of the water in St. Louis: it left a lot to be desired in 1904. I can remember my grandmother's describing a big barrel that she kept in the basement of her home at the turn of the century. Each night she would fill it with muddy Mississippi water, let it settle during the night and then the next morning, from above the muck, she would draw off fairly clear water for her family to drink that day. Not too long ago, one of our weekend newspapers made this statement about the drinking water in St. Louis in 1904: ''It was a little too thick to drink, but it was a little too thin to plow.'' It must have been pretty bad!

So, very early the question arose among the Fair Fathers, ''What in the world will we do about water on the Fairgrounds?'' Somebody had a bright idea and suggested, ''Let's bring it up in tank cars from the deep clear wells of DeSoto, roll the cars onto the Fairgrounds, ice the water and sell it for a penny a glass.'' The Fair Fathers dismissed any further worry about the water until they saw the beauty of the Cascades. Then they said, ''Oh, no, we can't have that beauty destroyed by having muddy water tumbling down there.'' The engineers were then *told*—they were not *asked*, ''Can you? Will you?''—but *told*, ''We *must* have clear water by the opening day of the Fair.''

Facing page, left: *A view of several statues in the Terrace of States. By comparing the size of the women on the stairs with that of the statues, one can get an idea of the statues' enormous size.*

Facing page, right: *The central Cascades were known as the Fountain of Liberty and the side Cascades were known as the Atlantic and Pacific Oceans, symbolizing "liberty extended from ocean to ocean by the purchase of the Louisiana Territory."*

Festival Hall (behind it stands the Palace of Fine Arts on the left), the eastern half of the Terrace of States, and the East Pavilion. The East Pavilion housed a German restaurant which was a favorite of the people of St. Louis.

35

To the left of the East Pavilion is the German building—a faithful replica of the famous Charlottenburg Castle, located outside Berlin.

36

Behind each of the four pairs of 140-foot obelisks outside the Palace of Mines and Metallurgy was an enormous globe (30 feet in diameter) supported by human figures 28 feet high each.

The entrance and obelisks of the Palace of Mines and Metallurgy. The figures at the bases of the obelisks give an idea of the scale of the palace.

Just a month before the Fair opened, at the end of March, St. Louis had clear water. It is ironic that it wasn't the drinking water that forced St. Louis to get clear water, but the Cascades!

With Festival Hall on our left, looking over to our right, we would see part of the Terrace of States—seven statues going to the west, seven going to the east—a total of fourteen. Each statue represented one of the states or territories carved from the Louisiana Territory. The terrace of seven statues going to the west ended in a pavilion called the West Pavilion, from which more cascades tumbled down. At the end of the other seven statues of states was the East Pavilion, which also had cascades—making three sets of cascades tumbling down Art Hill. But the Cascades before Festival Hall were the largest and most impressive.

The West Pavilion housed the Italian Cafe, which seated *2500* people. What restaurant do we have in St. Louis today that seats 2500 people? "Well," you might say, "maybe that was the *only* big restaurant on the Fairgrounds." But it wasn't. There were five restaurants on the Fairgrounds that could each seat over 2000 people, four could seat over 1500, six could seat 1000, and only 35 restaurants seated as few as 100 people. These restaurants could serve a sit-down meal to 36,650 people at a time.

Going down the east avenue, the Avenue of Orleans, the first palace we would see would be the Palace of Mines and Metallurgy, easily identified by its huge

The Sunken Gardens, with the Palace of Mines and Metallurgy on the right and the Palace of Liberal Arts on the left. The United States government building is in the background.

The Palace of Liberal Arts at night. In preparing the site for this palace, a ¼ mile-long lake had to be drained and filled.

obelisks. Here was the mining gulch—practical, working object lessons of the methods and machinery used in the sinking and operation of mines. Workers were actually mining coal. They dug an ore mine, also; they didn't strike ore, but there it was, full-size and working. The same with an oil well—full-size and working, but not producing oil. The Congress that met in this palace perfected the briquette and promised the elimination of smoke. How far ahead of their times they were!

While going from Mines and Metallurgy to the next palace, we would cross through one of the outstanding beauty spots of the Fairgrounds, the Sunken Gardens. Here the gardeners outdid themselves, for there was never a drooped flower or a dead leaf during the entire seven months of the Fair. The Gardens were literally a riot of color the entire time. Crossing through the Sunken Gardens, we would next see the Liberal Arts Palace, which exhibited typesetting and printing. It even contained a complete publishing plant that published a magazine about the Fair. These magazines can still be found in the library of the Missouri Historical Society and, I assure you, they read better than any historical novel.

In this building there also was a complete hospital, with patients, doctors, nurses, and equipment. Here the scientists in this field carried on low-temperature research. Our federal government was so impressed with the things these scientists were discovering that they hired the entire group (from all over the world) and, after the Fair, moved them and all their equipment to Washington, where they could continue their research.

In addition to the complete publishing plant and the complete hospital, the Palace of Liberal Arts also contained an auditorium which seated 60,000 people. Busch Memorial Stadium seats 55,000. Can you picture a building of wooden construction which would cover our stadium, plus seats for 5000 more, plus a hospital, plus a publishing plant?!

Now, going down the west avenue, the Avenue of St. Anthony, the first palace we would see was the Palace of Machinery, identifiable by its huge towers. Here we could see the latest advancement in the process of power generation—steam from coal (through boilers and engines) to electric generators. Next to this beautiful palace was a rather plain building which was called the Steam, Gas and Fuel Building. Each day coal cars from the coal mines of Missouri would dump 500 tons of coal here. That's how much it took to run the Fair for one day!

The eighth and last of the main palaces was the Palace of Transportation, which had huge entrances 60 feet high. This was the beginning of the era of the auto. There had been none at the Chicago Fair of 1893, but for our Fair 140 autos (some valued at $18,000) were driven under their own steam (or whatever their power was at the time) from Boston, New York, Chicago and

Six German steeples, each 285 feet high, gave a sense of solidarity and strength to the Palace of Machinery.

The Palace of Transportation, one of the largest palaces, contained 14 railroad tracks which extended from one end of the building to the other, for a total of 14 miles of tracks.

One of the three miniature trains that ran on the Fairgrounds. One train ran for one mile alongside the Pike. A second ran along Olympian Way (Forsyth), and the third served the Philippine reservation on the side nearest the Agriculture Building.

Philadelphia. Transportation at the Fair? Well, you name it, and they had it—from all over the world. One could ride in roller chairs and zebu carriages, on camels and turtles, in Irish jaunting cars and all kinds of gorgeous oriental equipages, or on burros, in dirigibles, or balloons. Transportation on the lagoons consisted of motor boats and gondolas; some of these were shaped like Cleopatra's barge, some like swans, and some like serpents' necks. Even the gondoliers were imported, to serenade Fair-goers as they rode.

Let me give a few more examples of transportation at the Fair. There were three miniature trains. (Wouldn't it be fun if we could find one, or several, of those trains to add to our Zoo collection? But, apparently, they are all long gone.) Then there was the electric bus—quite different from our buses today, but remember, this was a first. In 1904 few people had even ridden in a "horseless carriage" which seated four or five people—but here was a *big* horseless carriage that held twelve to fourteen people. The people loved it and, believe me, they used it.

All the World Was Here

The Pike was a storybook land. There were many fascinating things to see and do, including the "Battle of Santiago," the "Blarney Castle," the "Galveston Flood," the "Naval Battle," and "Under and Over the Sea."

Women wore "maxis" in those days and must have kept the Avenue of the Pike swept clean with them. (The Pike always seemed to be spotlessly clean.) In the background can be seen the "Tyrolean Alps."

The intramural train, which ran at the terrific speed of 12 miles an hour, did a 6½-mile circle tour of the Fairgrounds. The fare was ten cents. (The fare could be ten cents because motor men and conductors were paid only twenty-three cents an hour.) As the train was speeding west, roughly along Lindell, on the right would be the Pike.

The Pike was a living color picture of the world. It had concession buildings, architecture, and scenery of the world, from Japan to the Tyrolean Alps, from Siberia to the Cliff Dwellers. There was a statue of Teddy Roosevelt made of butter and a bear made of prunes.

On the Pike we would come to "Creation." I made the statement earlier that everything on the Fairgrounds was "for real." Well, naturally, they could not have a "for-real" creation of the world! But, after one of my first shows, a man came up to me and said, "After hearing you say that, I just had to tell you this. I was in that building and I sat through creation. After I sat through it one day at a time—Monday, Tuesday, Wednesday, Thursday, Friday, and Saturday—I really felt as if I had been there." So they must have done a terrific job!

The Pike also exhibited incubators. Of course, the people of St. Louis knew about chicken incubators,

"Creation" was a spectacular illusion based on the description in Genesis. Fair-goers glided along a water canal while a voice told the story. The first spectacle was that of chaos, followed by the appearance of light, then water and earth, then the sun, moon, trees, shrubs, and animals. The appearance of the first man and woman completed the effect.

The "Tyrolean Alps" had many houses with queer gables and towerlets. There was a hall where scenes from the Oberammergau Passion Play were shown. Tyrolean musicians played and singers yodeled. It would have taken hours to see all the wonders!

The interior of the St. Louis Inn. The day that President Roosevelt was in town, a banquet was held for him here; it is said that there was so much to eat that it took two hours to consume it!

After the Fair the building on the right was moved to the Forest Park Highlands, where it was used as the bandstand until it burned down a few years before the Highlands was demolished to build Forest Park Community College.

The sign, *"Our Theatre Heated,"* on the Irish Theatre made me wonder—What about the summer of 1904?
The average temperatures reported by the U.S. Weather Bureau were: May—66.1, June—75.4, July—
79.4, August—77.6, September—70.2, October—62.2, and November—53.3.

but they had never heard of, much less seen, baby incubators. Yet here they were, with one baby in each incubator tended by its own nurse and fed on its own individual schedule. The people really loved it!

The Pike also had an exact replica of the Tyrolean Alps. Another man came up to me after a show and said, "I had just come back from the Tyrolean Alps. Two days later I went to the Fair. I stopped dead in my tracks. I couldn't believe that I wasn't, by some miracle, again seeing the real thing." The finest inn on our Fairgrounds was located here; called the St. Louis Inn, it was a faithful copy of a famous inn in the Tyrolean Alps. I can still hear my Dad saying, "There never was food like Tony Faust served." Tony Faust catered the food for the St. Louis Inn, so it must have been outstanding. A young lariat- and chatter-man entertained patrons while they dined—none other than Will Rogers.

The Irish Theatre was such fun. People said there was a young tenor there with a voice the likes of which they had never heard before. His name was John McCormack. Between shows some of the Irish actors and actresses would come out to drum up trade for the next show and, of course, the Irish can be such fun!

Hagenbeck's Circus was another love of the Fairgoers. Yes, there were all kinds of wonders on the Pike! One could see a snowstorm and go ice skating daily. (We must remember that not only was this 1904, but also that these events occurred during the summer!)

Actors in front of the Irish Theatre between shows.

51

Hagenbeck's Animal Circus featured continuous performances of trained animals from noon until late at night.

A forerunner of modern zoos, Hagenbeck's allowed the animals to roam at large, as they would in a natural setting.

My dad never showed this picture without laughing. He loved seeing the clumsy old elephants slide down the narrow "shoot the chutes" and tumble into the tiny pool at the bottom. And the elephants loved it!

After the "Boer War," the "dead and dying" would get up from the battlefield, throw their arms around each other, and walk off the battlefield, only to return later and fight the war all over again.

The Siam Building, typical of buildings of the "Land of the White Elephant," was formally opened by David R. Francis with a golden key sent by the Crown Prince of Siam. To the left of the Siam Building are the pavilions of Nicaragua and Brazil.

There was a model garbage disposal plant with no odor, and people would stand around for hours saying, "There's got to be some odor to come out sometime," but it never did! There was Paris with its Bastille, guillotine, Montmartre, and Moulin Rouge. In addition, one could go through all kinds of illusions: through a cyclone, a whirlpool, or a submarine voyage; one could see the actual workings of a theatre, plus Ben Hur's chariot race; the Boer war was fought twice a day.

We must move on to the Terrace of Nations. Forty-five nations sent buildings. The Siamese Pavilion contained a collection of ancient weapons, musical instruments and models of temples from the Royal Museum of Bangkok. The French exhibit was a reproduction of the Grand Trianon, including gorgeous tapestries and elegant French furniture. Alex DeMenil, of St. Louis' own DeMenil family (whose home has been restored on the near south side), was there to see that the French exhibits were properly executed. St. Louisans especially loved the espalier trees, for they had never seen these before. And since the Fair took six years to build, the French gardeners had a chance to bring their fruit trees here, plant them, train them into their fantastically beautiful flat shapes against a house or trellis, and have them actually producing fruit by the time of the Fair.

The Japanese Garden was another outstandingly beautiful exhibit. The Japanese gardeners brought

The interior of the French Pavilion, which was a reproduction of the Grand Trianon at Versailles. It fronted on University Way (Skinker) and was set in a luxurious 15-acre garden.

The Gardens of Japan contained seven large buildings and many pagodas. Native materials (tiles, carvings, stone lanterns, etc.), as well as carpenters, gardeners, and other skilled workers, were brought from Japan.

The British Pavilion looked very much like the Linnaean House which stands in Shaw's Garden. (The Linnaean House was built by Shaw in 1881.)

their tiny bonsai trees, some of which were over 200 years old. The geisha girls were here and performed the authentic tea ceremony, dancing and singing in their soft, sweet voices.

The British Pavilion, a reproduction of the Orangery, Kensington Gardens, London, was on the Washington University campus, a little to the west of Skinker and north of Forsyth. After the Fair it was used as the Washington University Art School building until it was demolished to build the present building. It is interesting to note that the present art school building still has some of the exquisite fireplaces and interior trim saved from the British Pavilion.

Then, there was Jerusalem. This was one of the largest exhibits at the Fair, covering thirteen acres. It reproduced the Holy City of Palestine and embraced the most historic streets and buildings, such as the marketplace and the wailing wall.

Out on the Washington University campus, Francis Field (named for David R. Francis and built for the Fair) was the first concrete stadium ever built in the United States. And it's still in use today, some 70-odd years later. Do we build like this today? Apparently not. We seem to feel today that, "for business reasons," we must build for obsolescence. Now we seldom build for permanence.

Did you know that the third World Olympics were held in St. Louis for the Fair? The first World Olympics were held in Athens, the second in Paris, and the third in St. Louis. (In ten years I have found fewer than forty people who knew this. It is sad that many St. Louisans are unaware of their city's glorious past, and therefore find it difficult to take pride in its present or hope for its future.)

There is an interesting story about the Marathon. It was a hot day, as we sometimes have in St. Louis, and the Olympic course was about 26 miles long and very dusty. Beautiful Alice Roosevelt, daughter of President Teddy Roosevelt, was here to present a bouquet of red roses, as well as other prizes, to the winner. As the winner loped in, she stepped down from the platform and started a pretty little speech. But evidence was produced that the winner had gotten a ride along the way. (You see, they were cheating in those days, too!) Miss Roosevelt took the roses back and waited until the second runner came in. Frankly, I'm not so sure that he was entitled to it, either, for recently I read that "on his [the second runner's] last lap, his

Jerusalem, with more than a dozen closely-built streets, was a labyrinth of narrow passages that made a turbaned guide indispensable!

The start of the Olympic Marathon. 31 runners entered and 14 finished. There were 17 Americans, 10 Greeks, 2 Kaffirs, 1 Englishman (from South Africa), and a Cuban postman who had never run before.

handlers were giving him strychnine and brandy, and they were sponging him with water from their Stanley Steamer automobiles." I don't know whether he could have made it by himself!

The aeronautics section was intriguing. Remember, everything in the Fair was to be a learning experience. Since the Fair took six years to build, the Fair Fathers had time to get the word all over the world: "We have $100,000 for each contestant who can build anything that can fly with at least one person. We don't care what it is—a flying kite, a dirigible, or a balloon—just so it can get airborne." In order to make it easier to get airborne, an aeronautics field was built, with a 30-foot-high wooden fence around it to keep the wayward winds from blowing the contestants off course. Many came and tried. Few were successful. One of the most successful was a young flyer named Roy Knabenshue. He took off from the aeronautics field, cleared the fence, sailed off into the wild blue yonder and landed in Busch's Grove at Clayton and Price Roads. This was unheard of! The diners there were so excited that they rushed out and carried the flyer in on their shoulders. The bartender even created a drink in his honor; one can still go to Busch's Grove today and ask for a "Roy Knabenshue" and get the drink that the bartender originally created. (I tried it, and it's not bad!)

The Department of Anthropology presented the story of civilization, from the pygmies to the man-eaters to the Patagonian giants. The Fair Fathers did everything thoroughly: they didn't bring just a few natives from each tribe; they brought entire villages, however many families it took to make up that particular village. There were more than fifty tribes represented here, including the Igorots—headhunters from the Philippines. Some of the tribes were dog-eaters. Up until several years ago I did not know whether these tribes ever got real dogs to eat or whether they had to be satisfied with hot dogs (which were a first on the Fairgrounds). I have since learned that they were given dogs, furnished by the city dog pound. Either the quality or the quantity didn't quite satisfy the dog-eaters, because dogs from homes around the perimeter of the Fairgrounds were soon disappearing; when your pet didn't come back quickly, you could be pretty sure that it had landed in the soup kettle.

The people of St. Louis were charmed when they learned that the Negrito chief was going to be married on the Fairgrounds and that he had invited all of them to his wedding. That is, they were delighted until they learned that this was to be wife #3, and that wives #1 and #2 were with him!

One of the first things the Fair Fathers had to do for the tribes was to provide water because in their native habitats, most tribes naturally lived around water. Very early in their planning the Fair Fathers saw the need for a huge lake, which they called Lake Arrowhead. It was built on what we know as Wydown Boulevard, roughly where the Wydown School is today. (The football team of the Wydown School is still called the Igorots.) The tribes were brought from their respective countries with materials to construct their native habitat and mode of transportation. After the Fair, while excavating foundations for the mansions on Wydown Boulevard, workers unearthed some rather bizarre relics.

Some of the Samal Moros lived in stilt houses; other Moros were tree dwellers. The first time my grandsons became aware of this they said, "Gee, Grandma, we sure wish we could have had a *real* treehouse instead of the junk we threw together and *called* a treehouse." There were American Indians with their tepees and Indian mounds. (There *were* real Indian mounds in Forest Park, on the present golf course.)

The Igorot village housed more than a hundred spirit-worshiping members of three tribes. Tattooing was common with some of these people. The men used tattoos to record lives they had taken and the women used tattoos to enhance their charms.

Five widely different classes of natives from the Philippines were seen at the Fair. They ranged in degrees of civilization from the Negritos (seen here), who were so primitive that they had no fixed habitation, to the Visayans, whose culture was equal to the finest in America.

Some of the Moro tribes lived in stilt houses over either water or land. Others were tree dwellers.

The encampment of American Indians was composed of about 200 people from various government reservations.

This was my dad's favorite picture. He wanted badly to photograph this native, but couldn't communicate with him. Dad walked slowly toward the native, holding out the camera and going through the motions of taking a picture, until he thought he saw a glimmer of recognition on the native's face. Then Dad dug into his pocket and held up a nickel, saying, "If you let me take your picture, I will give you a nickel." There was silence for what seemed an interminable time. Finally, the native vigorously shook his head and in rising crescendos said, "No, no, no! Two nikkus, two nikkus!" The natives learned to bargain while at the Fair!

So Many Amazing Things

The Ferris Wheel (or Observation Wheel) carried the visitor to a height of 264 feet, giving him a constantly changing view of everything within the Fairgrounds and far beyond.

Through the Japanese Gardens could be seen one of the true wonders of the Fair—the Ferris Wheel or, the Observation Wheel. It was invented for the Chicago World's Fair by a young engineer named George Washington Gale Ferris (thus, the name "Ferris Wheel"). His fellow engineers laughed at him. They booed him and said, "Man, you're crazy! You'll never get that built. And if by any happenstance you do get it built, it will never run!" But Ferris did get it built. The Ferris Wheel ran throughout the Chicago Fair, then was dismantled, brought to St. Louis, and reassembled. It then ran throughout our Fair. It was unbelievably huge—264 feet high. (That's taller than the Railway Exchange Building.) It weighed 4200 tons. There were 36 cars, each of which seated 60 people. That meant 2,160 people could be moved in one revolution. Some friends returning from Vienna told me, "Hah, they have one just like it in Vienna." I suppose the Ferris Wheel in Vienna does look just like the one for the Fair, but when I looked up the statistics I read that the Vienna cars seat 30 people, while ours seated 60. Naturally, everything else had to be in like proportion.

One could even get married on the Ferris Wheel. One day after a show, a dear old lady came up to me and said, "I was married at the Fair." I said, "By any chance, were you married on the Ferris Wheel?" She clapped her hands and said, "Yes, yes, how did you know?" "Well, I didn't know that you were married on the Ferris Wheel," I replied, "but I do know that the Fair Fathers, with all their inventiveness, would lease out cars on the Wheel. People could lease a car and have a wedding, a dinner, a game party, or whatever they wanted."

It seems that, with all their imagination, the Fair Fathers could have thought of something to do with the Ferris Wheel after the Fair besides dynamiting it. But that is what they did! I think that if they had kept it, perhaps we would not have needed to build the Gateway Arch—who else would have had a Ferris Wheel like that?

The intramural railroad had seventeen small stations scattered over the Fairgrounds—travelers could get on and off at will. Getting off at Station 8 we would walk between the buildings of Ceylon and Canada, up to the Floral Clock. The Floral Clock was huge and beautiful. It was 112 feet in diameter, and its great hand weighed 125 pounds. The central portion consisted of verbena; the groundwork of the outer circle was centaurea; and the hour numbers, which were fifteen feet high, were coleus. The clock's performance was remarkably accurate. On one side of the little white pavilion at the top was a huge bell, which weighed seven thousand pounds and was amazingly accurate in tolling the hour and the half hour; the doors of the little white pavilion would open and one

Fair-goers flocked to ride in the huge cars of the Ferris Wheel. One ride, four huge revolutions, cost 50c. The revenues from the Ferris Wheel during the first four months of the Fair completely covered the costs of bringing it to St. Louis.

Doctor Arthur Proetz was a well-known ear, nose and throat doctor in St. Louis who wrote delightful things about old St. Louis. At the time of the Fair he was a student at Washington University. When the Ferris Wheel was dynamited at the end of the Fair, Dr. Proetz wrote: "It was like watching the execution of an old friend. When the dynamite went off under its base, the world seemed to stand still for a tragic moment as it shuddered, crumpled and sank slowly to the earth."

Station 8 of the intramural train is in the foreground. Between the buildings of Ceylon (left) and Canada (right) is the Floral Clock. The Agriculture Building is in the background.

*The Floral Clock had a minute hand that was 74 feet long and moved 5 feet every minute.
The face of the clock was clearly marked into one-minute intervals.*

75

could see the myriads of little wheels going round and round to make the clock work. On the other side of the pavilion was a huge hourglass, a magnification of the small three-minute hourglass that some of us use today for soft-boiled eggs. That, too, was remarkably accurate in turning on the hour.

Passing the Floral Clock, we would come to the Agriculture Building, the largest building on the Fairgrounds. Of wooden construction, it covered twenty acres under one roof. I would like to find a farmer who has a twenty-acre farm so that I can go out and pace off this distance, if I'm able, and try to imagine twenty acres under one roof. In the Agriculture Building could be seen the improvement in agricultural machinery, and the magnitude and variety of products. A Missouri farm was shown in three stages: cultivation, fruition and harvest. There was also a model dairy, a cider mill, a rice mill, a Parisian bakery, and an English bakery and confectionery. A dear friend, Dena Lange, as a schoolgirl in 1904, was intrigued with the Fair and went every chance she had. She didn't always have money left over for food, so sometimes she was hungry. When she learned that free samples of food were given away in the Agriculture Building, she was then able to dine—free of charge—on French pastries and English confections.

The Federated Women's Clubs of the United States, who started the warfare against food adulteration, held a Congress in the Agricultural Building. They actually tested brands and found two thousand brands that were adulterated. Jars of candy contained poisonous dyes. (We still have that problem today.) "Orange" phosphate never saw an orange. (We still have that today.) The women's Congress exposed so many things that they were warned to "lay off" or *else*! But the group was not stopped so easily. They went right ahead and demanded legislation to secure purity, true labeling, no chemical preservatives, and no coal tar dyes. This battle is still being fought today, seventy-five years later.

A permanent art building was built for the Fair because the countries of the world refused to send their best art treasures unless they were housed in a permanent building. It had an east wing and a west wing, but both were built of staff and were demolished after the Fair; then permanent east and west wings were built. The entire exhibit here was truly a reflection of the activity, progress, and position of the world's countries for all the branches of art.

At the southeast corner of the Fairgrounds were the buildings of the states. The Missouri Building was one of the most beautiful buildings on the Fairgrounds, and was built for permanence. It had a refrigerating plant in the basement so that the temperature could be kept in the seventies, even when it was in the nineties outside. The dome was 43 feet in diameter and, like the dome on Festival Hall, was covered with gold leaf. Inside the dome were paintings

The entrance to the Palace of Fine Arts (now the Art Museum) was (and is) decorated with a statue called "Painting" by Louis Saint-Gaudens, and a statue called "Sculpture" by Daniel C. French.

of the history of Missouri, symbolizing her progress in science, poetry, and art. We were to have kept this building but, unfortunately, on November 19 there was a disastrous fire and it was demolished beyond any hope of restoration. On this spot today stands a building known as the World's Fair Pavilion. Ninety-nine out of one hundred people think that because it's called that, it was built for the Fair. It was not! What *was* there was the beautiful Missouri Building. Don't let anyone tell you that the World's Fair Pavilion was part of the Fair!

Most state houses were copies of a historic building in that state. For instance, Jefferson's Monticello represented Virginia, Washington's headquarters at Morristown represented New Jersey, and Jackson's Hermitage represented Tennessee.

Circling back toward our starting point, we would pass the Bird Cage. Built by the Smithsonian Institution for the Fair, the Bird Cage had walkways through the center (which were restored several years ago). A little to the west of the Bird Cage is a large bronze plaque which states that when the cage was built for the Fair, the people of St. Louis loved it so much that they went to the city fathers saying, "Look, you've been talking about a zoo, so let's get going." The Bird Cage was, therefore, probably a big factor in the establishment of our world-famous St. Louis Zoo.

Having circled around almost to our starting point, we would see the Wireless Tower—an immense shaft

The Missouri Building had balconies at two levels, one 30 feet above the other. The top balcony, surrounding the base of the dome, was 130 feet above the ground. This building was intended to be permanent, but it was destroyed by fire on November 19, 1904.

The Bird Cage (U.S. Bird Exhibit) as it appeared during the Fair.

The Wireless Tower (background), with the Palace of Manufactures on the left and the Palace of Liberal Arts on the right.

Looking northwest from the Wireless Tower over the Model City and the Tyrolean Alps.

300 feet high. This was the point from which were sent the messages to Springfield, Chicago and Kansas City that were mentioned earlier. The tower also contained an electric elevator. Fair-goers had the thrill of riding 300 feet into the air and having a beautiful panoramic view of the Fairgrounds. After the Fair this tower was purchased by the St. Louis Traction Company (a forerunner of Bi-State), dismantled, and re-erected at Creve Coeur Lake, where, until taken down in 1932, it gave visitors to the lake the thrill of riding up 300 feet into the air.

So, having completed our tour of the Fair, we come to closing night—midnight, December 1, 1904. One hundred thousand people were there with David R. Francis and the Fair Fathers, waiting and mourning the closing of their Fair. Exactly at midnight David R. Francis closed the Fair with these words: "By bringing together hereto remote and unacquainted peoples, and thereby promoting mutual respect, the Fair was an important step toward establishing that universal peace for which all right-minded people are striving. Farewell, a long farewell to all thy splendor." And with those words he pressed a plunger which threw the entire Fairgrounds into darkness. Then came Pain's fireworks. You think we see fireworks today? We haven't seen anything! The fireworks created by Pain for the seven months of the Fair were unbelievable. On closing night he created the word "farewell" in fireworks across the sky, then the word "goodbye," then a recognizable portrait of David R. Francis, all in fireworks. The band played "Auld Lang Syne."

Thus ended an exposition that was a complete record, in actual reproductions, of the world at the turn of the century. An exposition that could be and should be a challenge to St. Louisans today—a challenge in leadership, in vision, in dedication, and in accomplishment!

Closing night, December 1, 1904, as seen from the Wireless Tower looking over the Palace of Manufactures and the Palace of Education and Social Economy toward Festival Hall. It took 6,600,000 candlepower to light the entire Fairgrounds.

Fabulous fireworks for the entire seven months of the Fair were created by the Pain Pyrotechnic Company of New York.

And Still More

The Louisiana Purchase

Robert R. Livingston, United States minister to the court of Napoleon, carried on the negotiations and accepted the offer of the entire Louisiana Territory for $15 million. Even after this decision, it took many ceremonies to finalize the purchase.

On April 30, 1803, Livingston was joined in Paris by James Monroe, a special envoy of President Jefferson. These men and Francois Marbois, Marquis de Barbè, signed the treaty which officially ceded the territory to the United States.

The Lower Louisiana Territory was officially transferred from Spain to France on November 30, 1803, at the Cabildo in New Orleans. On December 30, again at the Cabildo, the French flag came down, and the Lower Louisiana Territory became a part of the United States.

Eighty days later, in St. Louis, Captain Amos Stoddard of the United States Army effected the transfer of the Upper Louisiana Territory. Captain Stoddard wrote, "I took possession of the Upper Louisiana Territory in the name of France [from Spain] on March 9, and the next day I assumed the Country and the Government in the name of the United States." On March 10, 1804, the remainder of the Louisiana Territory became part of the United States, completing the transfer begun by the signing of the treaty ten and a half months earlier.

Dedicated to Accomplishment

World's Fair "pilgrimages"—The first "invasion of the empire" occurred from May 5 to May 15, 1901. Merchants, manufacturers and bankers, determined to win support for the Fair at all costs, rode a special, luxurious Missouri Pacific train as far away as Texas. No village was too small for a stop.

Unusual publicity—All traveling salesmen from St. Louis had the words "St. Louis World's Fair 1903" written in large, plain, white letters on their sample cases. Labels on trunks and manufacturers' packing cases also carried these words. Letters from as far away as Persia, Rome, Scotland and Japan came, asking for more information.

Press and publicity—50 trained, successful newspapermen worked closely together, flooding local papers with daily releases and sending weekly newsletters to thousands of newspapers (some in Central and South America). To check their response, they used a clipping service which returned 12,000 articles from non-St. Louis papers —"probably not $\frac{1}{10}$ of what appeared!"

The press—52,706 journalists came, saw, and wrote about the Fair. Representing newspapers from around the world, their coverage was "fair, discriminating, just and [would] insure its [the Fair's] lasting glory."

Exhibitor's fee—Exhibitors were not charged for either space or power in any of the beautiful palaces. (Yet this was the only World's Fair that has made money!)

Laborers' camps—Early in 1902, tent villages were erected in various parts of the grounds. The villages were identified by the contractors' names.

Washington University buildings used for the Fair—
Busch Hall—the Department of Works Building
Brookings Hall—the Administration Building
Cupples I—the Anthropology Building
Cupples II—used by the Jefferson Guard
Cupples Engineering Laboratory (torn down in 1967)—a warehouse for the Fair
Liggett Hall (now called Prince Hall)—a dormitory during the Fair
Ridgley Building—the Hall of International Congresses; also used to display Queen Victoria's Diamond Jubilee gifts
Power Plant—supplied power for the Exposition from 1902-1905; boasted the largest Gothic smokestack in the world
Lee Hall (originally Tower Hall, now Umrath Hall)—a dormitory
Francis Gymnasium and Francis Field
Eads Hall—the Board of Lady Managers Building

Aisles in palaces—The aisles in all the eight main palaces totaled 142 miles!

Board of Lady Managers—On March 3, 1901, a special act of Congress "appointed a Board of Lady Managers—one to be appointed on each committee authorized to award the prizes for exhibits produced in part or wholly by women." For the first time, a World's Fair operated entirely on a competitive basis, without regard to race, color or sex.

Dedication Day activities—Dedication Day was actually a three-day festival, continuing from April 30 through May 2. May 1 was "Diplomatic Day": a long parade of carriages, filled with diplomats and accompanied by mounted troops and bands, went from the Planter's Hotel downtown to the Washington U. campus, where lunch for 500 was served in the Hall of Congresses. May 2 was "State Day," devoted to the dedication of state building sites by the governors, state delegations and troops present. The day began with breakfast at the University Club, and was followed by parades and pageants. Pain's fireworks highlighted the three-day festival.

Dedication Day fireworks—Pain worked for months to prepare a preview in fireworks of Festival Hall, the Terrace of States, and the East and West Pavilions, along with the three Cascades. His large crew used giant-sized telephone poles as scaffolding to hold the colored fires outlining all the fireworks. During the day, 5000 hydrogen balloons were discharged; these were shaped like horses, elephants, frogs, etc. and made of fine tissue that inflated and floated to the ground.

Dedication Day parade—A favorite of St. Louisans, this parade covered all facets of the military and was two miles in length. The citizens enjoyed it so much that the Fair Fathers promised to duplicate it for Opening Day—and they did.

Russia bows out—As a result of Dedication Day, competition for exhibit space increased so much that the already extraordinary proportions of the palaces would have had to be multiplied three times to fill the demand. Then, just two months before Opening Day, Russia gave back the entire 80,000 square feet she had been allotted in many palaces. This space was quickly re-assigned in small sections to as many as possible (what a ticklish job that was!). But, what a scramble—to furnish plans, have them approved, then prepare, ship, install—all in two months! By working day and night in double shifts, the exhibitors made it. Remember their motto—"There is *nothing* we cannot and will not accomplish!"

Admissions—By dropping the correct coins in a turnstile, one could enter the Fairgrounds. All admissions were registered on dials in the Administration office, so that the number of admissions at each turnstile, as well as the grand total, could be known instantly. (And this was 1904!)

Roosevelt's reactions to the Fair—While President Roosevelt was here at the Fair (in November, 1903), someone asked him if he was having a good time. He replied, "My boy, I'm having the time of my life!"

Hotels built for the Fair included the Jefferson, Washington, Buckingham (later Kingsway), and the Epworth (once a home for senior citizens in University City, now for Washington University students) Hotels, the Outside Inn (Hamilton and Delmar), and the Inside Inn (built by Statler on the Fairgrounds near Oakland Ave.).

The Inside Inn was built by Col. E. M. Statler at a cost of $450,000. It covered ten acres, was three (and in some places, four) stories high, had nearly 3000 rooms (three times as many as the Waldorf Astoria), and employed over 1000 persons. By its second week 4200 guests had registered under either the European plan ($1.50 to $3.50 per day) or the American plan ($3 to $7 per day). Statler's life almost ended on Opening Day: when an ominous "boom" was heard in the hotel kitchen, Statler dashed in, only to be showered with boiling water from an exploding coffee urn. He was in critical condition for several days, but in two weeks was back at the hotel, directing the business from bed!

Trains from Union Station to the Fair consisted of ten cars, each seating 100 people. By running in a 1250-foot-block system, the trains were able to run safely one minute apart.

Railroads and streetcars could bring 80,000 people an hour to the Fair!

Opening Day services included a chorus of 500 at the Louisiana Purchase Monument singing "Hymn of the West," the official hymn of the Exposition, and also a parade of "picturesque peoples of the Pike."

The Opening Day Pike parade boasted peoples of sixty different tongues clad in native garb, animals from every clime, and vehicles strange to American eyes—gorgeous oriental rickshas, Irish jaunting cars, and zebu carriages.

The University of Man

Louisiana Purchase Monument—On the north side was a rostrum from which ceremonial speeches were delivered. On the south side was a group of statues (Livingston, Monroe and Marbois) shown signing the Louisiana Purchase treaty in Paris.

Palace of Manufacturers—The space in this palace for retail sales was divided into six-foot-square booths. For wholesale business, booths were larger.

The Model City housed a large part of the Social Economy displays. Here you would see model playgrounds, a model jail, a model town hall, and Salvation Army exhibits.

Palace of Electricity—One reporter called this building the "Wonder House." The "talking searchlight [radio phone]," he wrote, "was astonishing—it was connected with a telephone. The rays carried the voice which delivered the sounds into a concave mirror which focused them into the receiver held at the ear."

Thomas Edison's exhibit on the Fairgrounds contained his first electric locomotive and car, his dynamo (1881), and his lamps, fixtures and meters. One of Edison's most recent inventions was the steel-nickel storage battery, designed especially for automobiles. An Edison battery weighing 500 lbs. took an automobile the 60 miles from Boston to New York in 48 hours (including all stops) without recharging. How times have changed!

The huge organ in Festival Hall was really five organs in one, but all could be played by one performer by means of connecting attachments. The player would sit at a movable console, his fingers commanding five manuals or keyboards, 140 draw-stop knobs, 46 pushbuttons, and all the foot levers. The organ had 10,159 pipes. (A Shetland pony was led into the largest pipe as it lay on the ground awaiting installation.)

Cascades—The pumping equipment for the Cascades (2000 horsepower) was sufficient to raise 90,000 gallons of water a minute to a height of 150 feet.

The lagoons and Grand Basin held 25 million gallons of water. The entire volume of water circulated once every five hours.

Statues along the Cascades—The pathway along the Cascades up to the West Pavilion was lined with statues of soldiers and statesmen; the path to the East Pavilion, with statues of explorers.

Food service—Eating places numbered 125. Of these, 45 were restaurants, the rest were "fast food" lunch stands. The Fair Fathers figured that 100,000 people could be fed simultaneously three times a day. The ice cream cone, the hot dog, and iced tea were introduced to the world at the Fair.

The German Building—The original Charlottenburg Schloss had been erected 200 years before by Frederick of Prussia. Its replica at the Fair had a great dome containing bell chimes that sounded the hours, as well as a golden maiden weathervane on the top. Inside, the castle was furnished with the original furniture that had been in the Charlottenburg for two centuries.

Vulcan statue—In the center of the Palace of Mines and Metallurgy stood the huge statue of Vulcan, sent by Alabama. Made of iron, the statue was 56 feet high and weighed 100,000 lbs. After the Fair the statue was moved to Birmingham on seven freight cars; today it overlooks that city from Red Mountain. In Vulcan's hand is a huge light which glows for 24 hours after every fatal accident.

The Palace of Liberal Arts had many fascinating exhibits: the British Mint's great coin collection, an extensive display of musical instruments, ancient books, carvings, armor, weapons, and rare trophies from Chinese temples.

Palace of Machinery—The "marvels of our industrial age" (just getting rolling in 1904) brought forth the rather prophetic statement that "human labor is at a discount, human ingenuity is supreme."

Locomotive tests in the Palace of Transportation accumulated an enormous mass of valuable engineering data on the relative merits of different locomotives: proportion of fuel consumed, speed developed, power exerted, friction of bearings, wear of machinery, etc. Many railroads exhibited at the Fair, and the American Society of Engineers helped the Department of Transportation with the planning.

Steam, Gas and Fuel Building—Inside this building the 500 tons of coal brought in daily would be dumped into bins, where automatic conveyors in the rafters would take the coal down to the automatic stokers, which in turn would carry it into the fire-boxes. The resulting ashes dropped into a pit beneath the floor. The steam made was piped underground from the boilers to the Palace of Machinery. No soot, ashes, or human labor was seen by the Fair-goers!

All the World Was Here

Strolling on the Pike—After the exhibit palaces closed at night, throngs of people would walk on the Pike, thrilling to the sights, the sounds, the amusements, and the entertainments—up to 100,000 people endlessly on the move!

The concessions on the Pike represented an investment of between $7 and $8 million.

Tyrolean Alps—One could take a tramcar trip through the mountains, stopping for glimpses of Alpine villages, including the birthplace of Mozart. At the end of the line an elevator could be taken to the peaks of the Ortler, where a waterfall tumbled down into a lake; across this lake was a church.

The Irish Theatre was in the Irish Village on the Pike. This village was a collective and truly national exhibition of Ireland's educational facilities and wants, and of present industrial conditions and possibilities. The entrance to the village was a very imposing facsimile of the exterior of the Irish House of Parliament in Dublin.

Fair Japan on the Pike—There were pretty tea houses, gardens with lakes and lagoons, a Japanese theatre, and a restaurant.

A *"permanent Pike"*—Some citizens hoped to establish the Pike permanently. Plans included an artificial beach large enough for 5000 bathers; an immense tower with 50,000 electric lights; a large stadium; and a model playground. Adolphus Busch purchased the Tyrolean Alps concession, hoping to combine it with a summer theatre. The "permanent Pike" idea was opposed by Washington University, as they felt the nearness of the Pike's attractions would be distracting to the students. The plans were abandoned.

The British Pavilion, at the intersection of Administration Ave. and University Way (Lindell & Skinker) was a replica of the Orangery, built for Queen Anne as the banquet hall of Kensington Palace. Designed by Sir Christopher Wren, it contained rooms typical of several different reigns: an Elizabethan room, a Queen Anne room, a Georgian room, and others with more recent furnishings.

The Ceylon Building could have been called the "Temple of the Teas," for at four o'clock the ladies flocked here to drink Ceylon's delicious teas, served in dainty cups decorated with pictures of Adam's Peak (according to native tradition, the "footstool" of the first man). The teas were served by solemn-faced Singalese men in skirts, their long hair curled at the back of the head and held in place by large tortoise-shell combs.

The Brazil Pavilion was a structure of unusual elegance, in which Brazil showed herself so rich and diversified in resources and industries as to astonish the public. Brazil also had extensive displays in seven buildings: Agriculture, Forestry, Mines and Metallurgy, Liberal Arts, Transportation, Education, and Fine Arts. The coffee display in the Agriculture Building covered 4641 square feet, and was almost surrounded by dozens of glass pillars, each a foot in diameter and filled with coffee beans.

China Building—Located where south Brookings parking lot is today, the China Building was one of the wonders of the Fair. A copy of the summer palace of Prince Pu Lun, it contained a wealth of Chinese art and artifacts, including jades, porcelains, bronzes, lacquered woods, silks, and ceramics. The Prince had such a marvelous time at

91

the Fair that he gave the entire pavilion and contents to David R. Francis personally!

The Olympics lasted from August 29 to September 3. Besides Francis Field and the Gymnasium, playing fields, running tracks and a "swimming hole" were constructed. A total of 9000 athletes from all over the world competed in 38 separate contests, and 3280 "turners" competed in calisthenics and tests of agility, skill, and strength. Many records were established: in the shot-put, a hairy Ainu from Japan heaved a 56-lb. weight 1 yd., 3 in. Pigmy mud fights and pole-climbing events were additional attractions to Fair-goers. (One Igorot shinnied up 50 feet in 20 seconds.)

Aeronautics course—Above the 30-foot-high fence surrounding the aeronautic course (which was roughly where Fraternity Row is on Washington U's campus today) was 18 feet of slat work, which could be covered with canvas as a windbreak.

Pygmies—These tiny, slender, and active persons, averaging 4 ft. 10 in. in height, were often mischievous, capricious and troublesome on the grounds. The Pygmies were all Ethiopians from south central Africa. Even in the time of Egyptian greatness, these small Negroes were feared because of their unerring aim and poisoned arrows.

The Negritos were exceptionally skilled with the bow and arrow. Shortly after the Fair opened, when the grounds were infested with sparrows, Fair officials sent these tribesmen to take care of the nuisance, which they did quite handily!

Chief Antonio of the Igorots insisted on having a telephone in his hut, as a distinction appropriate to his rank.

Dog-eating Igorots—Dr. T. K. Hunt, in charge of the tribes, asked the city pound to supply dogs for the Igorots. The Women's Humane Society, in emergency meeting, vigorously declared their opposition: "If they want dog meat, they can import it in cans!" Chief Antonio then petitioned Judge William H. Taft (later President Taft), who replied that the request was reasonable and thus approved the voucher. Dr. Hunt closed the deal, for a supply of twenty dogs a week. Chief Antonio, to express the tribe's gratitude, invited Mr. Taft to their feast—but the judge courteously declined!

"Patagonian Giants" of southern Argentina—The men averaged about six feet in height; the women just an inch or two less. The men were powerful, expert in horsemanship and in the use of bolas (the native weapon, formed by attaching three stone balls to leather thongs), one of the most effective of primitive weapons from southern Argentina.

Village of the Samal Moros—One day the village custodian took the Moro boys to the Pike, where, for the first time, they saw "shooting the chutes." They were so delighted that they couldn't wait for the boat to finish its course; they jumped into the water, scrambled up the incline and pleaded for more. The next day they tried to build a "chute" of their own with bamboo poles, with no success. The custodian came to the rescue, got planed boards, and a carpenter built a "chute" down which the boys' dugouts shot with great rapidity (usually capsizing and spilling), which in no way detracted from their new sport.

Enmity between Moros—The Samal Moros, who lived in stilt houses over water, were mainly sea rovers, pearl divers, and fishermen, but they were also experts in metal work and weaving. The Lanao Moros lived inland. There was fierce enmity between these two tribes and they were carefully separated.

American Indian tribes represented at the Fair—
Cocopa—from Lower California
Pawnee—from Kansas and Nebraska
Sioux—from North and South Dakota
Pima, Papago, Maricopa, Navajos, Apaches, Pueblo, Hopi—from Arizona
Arapaho—from New Mexico
Cheyenne—from the western plains
Kickapoo—from Kansas
Wichita—from Oklahoma

So Many Amazing Things

Canada Building—Designed for the comfort of Canadians and hospitality to all others, this building was a well-planned clubhouse, 100 feet square. Porticos, which surrounded the building, offered shelter and an interesting view. It was a convenient, comfortable half-way resting place.

Floral Clock—Everything connected with the Floral Clock was moved by compressed air, but it was all controlled by the delicate, accurate master clock, which was visible under glass. It was amazing to watch it tick off the minutes and then see it duplicated on the huge clock! Close to the clock was a terrestrial globe which revolved once every 24 hours, on which you could read the time of day at any place on earth.

The Agricultural exhibits covered all products coming directly or indirectly from the cultivation of the soil; the tools, implements, and methods used in planting; the entire growth process; manufactured forms and by-products; and the preparation of everything derived from land cultivation that entered into home life and commerce of the world.

Landscaping the Fair—60,000 shrubs, 9000 deciduous trees (not counting those already in the park), 1300 evergreens, 5000 vines, and 100,000 bulbs were planted. Thousands of century plants, which had become too large for the grounds of Notre Dame University, were brought here on railroad cars from South Bend, Indiana, and planted.

Outdoor horticultural displays included the plant map, a desert garden, a rose garden of 10,000 plants, and lakes covering two acres which exhibited rare and beautiful aquatic plants. Landscaping and gardening began three years before the Fair opened.

The Plant Map—Here each state of the U.S. was represented by its native plants and grasses—819 species. Gravel walks outlined the states and coasts. The five-acre map was underlaced with drains to carry off surplus water.

The Horticultural Building covered six acres and was directly behind the Agricultural Building. In its center were exhibits of fruits, nuts, and melons. There were two huge wings: the east wing was a conservatory for flower shows and for the exhibition of conservatory plants and rare exotics. The west wing exhibited cut flowers and horticultural implements. A rotunda 76 feet square was the principal interior feature. In the center was an electric fountain gushing ice water. An adjoining auditorium and reception room seated 1500 people.

Military pageants—One of the most notable military pageants of the Exposition was given at the Missouri Building by the West Point Cadets, here for their military commencement ball. They were housed in a Washington University dorm.

Missouri Building burns—A huge crowd watched silently as flames enveloped the beautiful structure. The U.S. flag, still waving over the west portico, suddenly fell to the ground as the flagpole gave way. Seeing that the flag was unharmed by the flames, the crowd gave a tremendous cheer. Some of the furniture from the Missouri Building was saved, and stands today in the Governor's mansion in Jefferson City.

The New Jersey House was a copy of the old Ford House at Morristown, which had been used by Washington as

winter headquarters during the Revolutionary War. After the Fair it was moved to Kirkwood on Bodley, just east of Kirkwood Road, and made into four lovely apartments. I visited one of these, a charming townhouse. I was appalled several years later to learn that it had been torn down. The house originally contained over thirty rooms.

Wireless Tower—Of the seven stations operated by the De Forest Wireless Telegraph Company on the Fairgrounds, the Wireless Tower located on the Plaza of Orleans attracted the most attention, not only because of its height, but also because of its demonstrations of wireless telegraphy. Messages could be sent a distance of 1500 miles over land, and even farther over water, giving promise of supplanting the Atlantic cable laid just 45 years before.

David R. Francis Day—The last day of the Fair, a day of continuous ovation to a remarkable man.

Miscellaneous

Democratic Party convention—The national Democratic Party convention of 1904 was held in St. Louis. Alton B. Parker was nominated as President of the United States.

Attendance—Total attendance at the Fair was 19,695,855. The average daily attendance was 100,000. At night there were usually 20,000 people on the Fairgrounds, including the tribal natives, workmen, custodians, Jefferson Guards, and guests at the Inside Inn.

The intramural railroad had seventeen stations. Tracks for these trains were sub-surface in some areas, street level in other areas, and slightly elevated in others.

Sewers and pipes—The Fairgrounds were laced with storm and soil water sewers; with drains for domestic water use; and with gas pipes and electrical conduits.

Fire protection—There were five firehouses and fourteen large fire pumps on the Fairgrounds.

Official Fair flag—The official St. Louis World's Fair flag consisted of a *fleur de lis* surrounded by fourteen stars on a field of blue, with three stripes (red, white and yellow) of equal width going to the right.

Solar power in 1904—A Portuguese priest at the Fair built a "sun machine," which could produce a heat of over 7000 degrees Fahrenheit.

Transportation Day water pageant—On the big lagoon could be seen all sizes, shapes and varieties of water transportation: besides the launches and gondolas, there were barges, rowboats, birch-bark and dugout canoes— hundreds of boats, all loaded with flowers and shrubbery. The St. Louis boat had a floral picture of a keg of beer and a pair of shoes, totally obscured by the people on the boat!

Social life 1904—Some of St. Louis' "upper crust" felt that the Fair would be nothing more than a noisy, vulgar show. They either closed their homes or rented them to foreign commissioners, and left for Bar Harbor. They rued the day! For the families who stayed, it was one party after another: 1600 bottles of champagne were consumed at one German party; the Chinese Commissioner's receptions were fabulous; and fortunes were spent on the French and Mexican parties. While the local elite consumed sour grapes from afar, socialites from other cities rushed to St. Louis. Houseboats with striped awnings, teakwood decks, and mahogany rails docked on our riverfront, and one day twenty private railroad cars shunted into the Wabash station on the Exposition grounds.

Concerts—There were six bandstands on the Fairgrounds, and each gave at least two concerts daily.

Demolition—Within six months after the Fair, Forest Park was to be "cleared of all tramways, railroad tracks, buildings, rubbish, debris, sheds, pavilions, and towers." Within twelve months the Exposition Company had to "fully restore the park to its original state."

David R. Francis said of St. Louis: "We need to have a certain narrowness of vision altered. We need to learn something of our own merits and possibilities, so that many of our own people will realize a little better than they do, that St. Louis is, in its way, as great a city as any on the continent."

A Final Thought

These words from an anonymous Fair-goer may help us to better understand St. Louis' lasting enthusiasm about the 1904 World's Fair:

"It is difficult now to express the wonder and the sense of awe we experienced when we first saw the Fair on Opening Day, April 30, 1904. Of course, we had seen it in construction, but on that perfect April day with the flags catching the breeze and the sound of music everywhere, we suddenly discovered that we were all very proud of our city—and, I suppose, quite foolishly proud of ourselves. We admired everything: the statues, the buildings, the fountains—the good and the bad. We liked it all!

"If you had to explain it, about all that you could say was that the people of St. Louis fell in love with their Fair.

"And, like travelers on a long and wonderful journey, we felt very close to one another. Strangers smiled at strangers and each person was, I'm sure, thinking of the summer to come—when there would be time to explore every rich detail, take every ride, and see everything there was to see at our wonderful, wonderful fair!"